I0786414

BIRTHDAY GIRL!

PARTY TIME!

Let's Celebrate!

TODAY IS THE DAY TO BE HAPPY!

YOU ARE AMAZING!

CHEERS!

IT'S YOUR SPECIAL DAY!

HIP! HIP! HOORAY!

IT'S YOUR BIRTHDAY
MAKE A WISH!

BELIEVE IN MAGIC!

YOU ARE AWESOME!

HAPPY
BIRTHDAY

HAPPY BIRTHDAY!
COLORING CARD

Copyright 2018
By Florabella Publishing, LLC
florabellapublishing@yahoo.com
All rights reserved. No part of this book
may be reproduced in any form or by
any electronic means including
information storage and retrieval systems,
without permission in writing from the
authors. The only exception is by a reviewer,
who may quote short excerpts in a review.

www.ingramcontent.com/pod-product-compliance
Lightning Source LLC
Chambersburg PA
CBHW070024260726
48658CB00003B/1035